An Evolution of Faith

by Richard L. Bigford

First Edition 2021

ISBN: 978-1-954666-03-0

Written for all the
John Does and Jane Does out there.
For those who are lost, not knowing
where they came from, where they're
going, and who they really are.

Richard L. Bigford

CONTENTS

Richard L. Bigford

Introduction

At times in my life I have considered myself a John Doe, lost, with no memory of who I really am, where I came from, and no real guidance of where to go, left to my own devices, so it seems. I've wandered the great highway of life, weaving through the traffic, trying to find my way home, changing and evolving according to my environment. Will I be the same person my Father knew when I return home as when I left?

Within these writings, I hope to shed light on your intellectual understanding of life eternal. Life is full of things we need to overcome and endure. We're better able to get to a destination if we have the particulars of where we're going, why we're going there, and how long it takes to get there. We need a road map of a road well-traveled by many.

Like this book, all things created on earth arrive from a spiritual beginning, such as the thoughts we have about creating anything. The ability to create something starts with an idea and is developed within our minds, where we use our imagination to see if our idea can or should be done. As our idea is tested, we receive confidence in our ability based on the action or reaction of the test. Good results create a positive outlook. Bad results can create a negative outlook if we let it. Both results make us more determined than ever to make our ideas or dreams come true.

A good example of this is the invention of the light bulb. The inventor didn't give up on his idea. Likewise, in life, we must never give up hope of a better life. We must be creative and challenge ourselves, not being afraid of the obstacles. If we know where we're going, we are sure to get there safely.

My hope is that you'll gain knowledge that will give you strength to press forward when there's no real end in sight, and that will help you endure to the end of this life while looking forward to the next life.

Throughout this text, I make references to my own thoughts and experiences in life and references to scripture from the King James Version of the Bible and the Book of Mormon: Another Testament of Jesus Christ. Please be sure to read the references for further understanding of the scripture passages that I summarize and expound upon. Then ponder and pray about what I say.

Richard L. Bigford

To Live or To Die?

When I was eleven years old, I became sick and found out I had cancer (Hodgkin's Lymphoma). Though I was sick, endured surgery to remove my spleen, and had had many tests, at no time did dying enter my mind. I was just sick, and the doctors took care of me.

Some of my stay at the hospital wasn't pleasant. One time, I got so tired of them taking blood from me. Three times a day was just too much! I saved a few snacks and went to the bathroom. I locked the door and stayed there for several hours until I ran out of snacks.

I got to see many other kids sick like me. My mother tried to keep me from doing too much, as if I was fragile and would break. I hated that! I did what I wanted to do. But that's what mothers did best—love and protect.

I was cured of the cancer because they caught it in stage one. Not all those who get cancer have a chance to live a long life. I often wonder why God let me live.

I must still have a special job to do.

In the Beginning

We might say that when life begins, evolution begins both in heaven and on earth.

According to what I've read from the scriptures, we started off in heaven as spirit children of our Heavenly Father, with great freedom and knowledge. But we lacked one thing to make us complete like our Father in Heaven.

We needed a body of flesh and bones.

Having a body would allow us to fully understand pain and pleasure. A body would help us find balance between these two drastically different emotions.

A Grand Council was convened in heaven where we discussed the final step of getting a body to become like our Heavenly Father. A great division arose of how and who should lead the way toward us receiving our bodies, with God being the final judge on the matter.

After God's decision, many were displeased, so much so that the great spiritual War in Heaven began (Revelation 12:7). Perhaps more of a war of words than a physical battle, leading to hatred and many other unspeakable events. Our Father had to step in and make the final say on who and how we were to receive our bodies. He ended the War in Heaven at a great cost.

Now the war on earth has begun! This time with our bodies that we need to develop both physically and spiritually.

Life on Earth

One third of the spirits in heaven were cast down to earth, never to receive the great blessing given to us from our Father, our bodies.

Those of us who followed God's plan in heaven came to earth to receive a body, to grow and develop both physically and spiritually, and further evolve into our true selves to eventually become like God.

We have the freedom to choose good or evil. The choices we make while on earth and how we evolve spiritually will determine our individual destinies. We will either return to heaven or get cast out to outer darkness.

But we will evolve! We are in a state of constant change whether we like it or not. Change is imminent and part of our plan for true happiness or misery.

Evolution
Both Physically and Spiritually

Evolution has been a source of debate throughout the times. The Webster Dictionary definition of the word evolution is described in three ways.

1. One of a set of prescribed movements.

This definition reminds me of making a specific compound in chemistry—combining different substances in a specific order to make a single new product.

Another, perhaps simpler to understand, example is baking. Several ingredients are added together in a specific order to make a final baked good, for example, bread.

2. A process of change in a particular direction.

Using the baking example from above, we have a plan to make banana bread. We have a particular direction, or destination, if you will, with a specific outcome in mind. We begin with bananas and other ingredients. Through a process of change to the involved ingredients, we end up with banana bread.

3. A theory that the various kinds of plants and animals are descended from other kinds that lived in earlier times and that the differences are due to inherited changes that occurred over many generations.

As for the many theories on the types of changes that have taken place over the years, one theory stands out—the theory on the evolution of man.

An Evolution of Faith

Why do we try to understand and prove evolution?

Because we all have a question inside us that we're dying to ask.

Where did we come from?

The John or Jane Doe inside us surfaces as more questions come, and we feel lost in a world of confusion and strife.

Darwin's hypothesis or theory of evolution grew into the idea that man evolved from apes. His idea was to prove physically where we came from for those unsatisfied with explanations in the Bible and other scriptural guidance of our existence and how we came to be.

Richard L. Bigford

So Who Are You?

Do you really know who you are?

As for me, I consider myself to be a child of God! I have been evolving into who I really am for fifty-four years, and I still don't understand the magnitude of my full potential. I hope that another fifty-plus years will help solidify the thoughts and feelings of my heart to shape me into who I'm meant to be. I say child of God!

But what does it really mean to be a child of God? Well, to me, just knowing the one simple fact that I am a child of God gives me direction. If I am God's child, then I know that I came from where He dwells. This gives me a place to

Richard L. Bigford

strive toward, with faith, hope, and knowledge for a better life in the future.

Faith and the Holy Ghost

Some people want to believe in God, but where is He in our need for guidance?

The scriptures require us to have faith in a being unseen by most. Faith is a hard concept to grasp for most people.

In the Bible we read, "Now faith is the substance of things hoped for, the evidence of things not seen" (Hebrews 11:1).

I would like to add to that definition of faith so that we might have a better understanding of how someone can have such strong faith in God and other things.

Richard L. Bigford

Faith is an action we perform when we experience feelings from either God or Satan. Truth from God. Lies from Satan. As a special messenger from God, the Holy Ghost testifies of the truthfulness of all things that come from God. On the opposite of that spectrum, Satan stretches the truth to the point that it becomes a lie. Without relying on the Holy Ghost, we can scarcely tell the truth from a lie created by Satan.

Faith is felt within the heart and not seen. That's why we can have faith in so many things. A good heart will have faith in good things. A bad or corrupted heart will have faith in bad things.

Who and what is the Holy Ghost? How do we discern the truth from a lie?

The Holy Ghost is one of our brothers from heaven. Just as Jesus is our older brother from heaven.

In the plan for our happiness, Christ was sent as a physical witness to earth. He received a body so that He could overcome death and satisfy the demands of justice for us. Otherwise, we would have to suffer for our own sins if someone didn't take the punishment. Thus we became subject to Jesus Christ's mercy and love for us all. Thus Christ became the mediator between us and God, showing us the way to return to God.

The Holy Ghost was also sent, without a body, and will not receive a body until his work is done. He was sent to be a spiritual witness of all truth that comes from God. He is a mass of potential energy, if you will, that is released when testifying of truth. When we seek out the truth, we can receive or feel His energy that connects His spirit to ours. That sensation we receive is often referred to as a feeling in the bosom.

I recently named this feeling "tears of the spirit." Lately I have done a lot of reflection on my life and have cried quite a bit. Thus the name "tears of the spirit."

The Holy Ghost has limitations. The Holy Ghost cannot dwell in an unclean temple, meaning the unclean temple of our bodies. Our temples are made of more than just our bodies though. Our temples are who we are. It encompasses our minds, bodies, and spirits. The cleaner the temple, the longer the capacity for the Holy Ghost to stay as a guest. If we make and keep certain covenants with God, such as covenants made through baptism, the Holy Ghost can and will become a more permanent resident in us to guide us and grow our knowledge in all things that are true. Keeping God's commandments and covenants will help us retain the companionship of the Holy Ghost.

How do we find the Holy Ghost to receive His guidance?

The Holy Ghost is everywhere that's good because there's truth in all things that are good. The trick is determining what's good and what's bad.

Humble yourself to ask God the Eternal Father in the name of His Beloved Son Jesus Christ. If you have a sincere desire to know the truth, the

An Evolution of Faith

Holy Ghost will testify of the truthfulness of all things you ask of Him. Humble prayer is the greatest way to communicate with God through the Holy Ghost.

My experience with the Holy Ghost is hard to explain, because we're all different and experience life in our own way.

I had not been taught anything about the Holy Ghost from my youth. I had to learn, as the scriptures say, "line upon line, precept upon precept, here a little and there a little" (2 Nephi 28:30). After I learned to study the scriptures daily and observed loving people willing to lift me when I needed help—showing me how a Christlike person should act—after I was taught the importance of prayer and how to pray and started to search, ponder, and pray, I gradually developed a connection with the Holy Ghost. I started to realize certain feelings. I would experience a burning in the bosom, and at times cry with such emotional power that I knew

Christ lived. The Holy Ghost has testified this to me through those special feelings of the heart.

We have to chase the Holy Ghost for knowledge about God! He's not going to chase us! Wanting to know more about God has to be a desire of our hearts.

An Evolution of Faith

Evolution is a Spiritual Journey

From a scriptural standpoint, let's look at our humble beginning in the plan of our happiness.

From the scriptures we read, "In the beginning God created the heaven and earth" (Genesis 1:1).

If we read, ponder, and pray as we read the scriptures, we understand that God's power created the heavens and earth and that God let angels, or rather certain children of His, create the earth under his direction and power.

> And God said, let the earth bring forth the living creature after his kind, cattle, and

creeping thing, and beast of the earth after his kind: and it was so (Genesis 1:24).

So God created man in his own image, in the image of God created he him; male and female created he them (Genesis 1:27).

All flesh is not the same: but there is one kind of flesh of man, another flesh of beast, another of fishes, and another of birds (1 Corinthians 15:39).

Apes came from apes, fish from fish, birds from birds, and man from man. This is a simple concept to understand.

The scriptures clearly state that God created us in His image, so if we believe that man evolved from apes, logically this concludes that we believe God is or has been an ape. But then none of this is true or matters if we don't believe in God or if we don't understand or haven't studied the scriptures.

An Evolution of Faith

Here's my take on evolution. It's a spiritual journey.

All things created on earth arrive from a spiritual beginning, much as thoughts that we have about making, creating, or performing a task do. The ability to create starts with an idea and is developed in our minds.

There are two ways to test whether we should attempt creation. One, build our concept to craft a physical manifestation or, two, envision our creation in our minds. As we test our idea, we receive confidence in our ability to create based on the test's action or reaction.

Good results give us a positive outlook. Bad results, a negative outlook. Both results make us more determined to create our ideas.

Many ideas can be created, but would the idea be bad or unethical? We should look at all aspects of creation. It should be for the good of mankind, not for the detriment of mankind.

God never created anything that didn't have a specific purpose and wasn't good for mankind.

Men and women evolve in two directions as they make choices in life. Remember that with every change, we will have a reaction to that change. We do good things and we feel good and want to be better. Good choices lead to righteousness, toward God. We do bad things and we feel bad and want to hide from the shame. Bad choices lead to evilness, toward Satan.

I made what I call *The Scale of Life* to illustrate what I said.

An Evolution of Faith

The Scale of Life

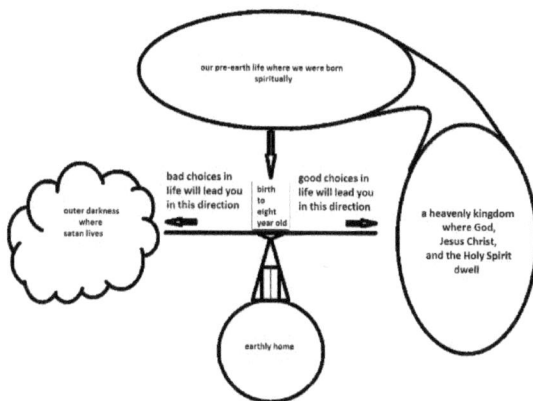

our pre-earth life where we were born spiritually

bad choices in life will lead you in this direction

good choices in life will lead you in this direction

birth to eight year old

outer darkness where satan lives

a heavenly kingdom where God, Jesus Christ, and the Holy Spirit dwell

earthly home

Richard L. Bigford

The First Example of Spiritual Evolution

To me, Adam and Eve are the first real example of spiritual evolution.

God sent our first parents Adam and Eve to earth.

We read that God created Adam's earthly body from the dust and breathed air into Adam and placed him in the garden east of Eden (Genesis 2:7, 8). Then God made Eve, a woman, from one of man's ribs (Genesis 2:21–23).

Adam and Eve were each given a body and placed into the Garden of Eden and were given freedom to evolve into their own spiritual persons. They had two choices. One was to rely solely on their Father's wisdom and knowledge to teach them all things and to become a spiritual being like God our Father. Or two, to evolve into a natural man, gaining wisdom and knowledge from divers spirits, relying on their own strength and wisdom. The one being good, the other having the potential of being good or being bad.

While in the Garden of Eden, Adam and Eve were given a commandment.

> And the Lord God commanded the man, saying, Of every tree of the garden thou mayest freely eat:

> But of the tree of the knowledge of good and evil, thou shalt not eat of it: for in the day that thou eatest thereof thou shalt surely die (Genesis 2:16–17).

The consequence of such disobedience would be death. Man would die or, rather, be subject to death.

An Evolution of Faith

The serpent, Satan, tempted the woman to eat of the tree of knowledge of good and evil, saying, "Ye shall be as gods, knowing good and evil" (Genesis 3:5). Eve ate the fruit and got Adam to eat also. At that point, changes began that allowed them to make choices according to whom they listened.

God learned that Satan beguiled the woman to partake of the tree of the forbidden fruit. So God punished Satan, putting enmity between "thee and the woman, and between thy seed and her seed" (Genesis 3:15) so that the serpent couldn't harm man and so that man would have power to overcome Satan.

God punished the woman. He said, "I will greatly multiply thy sorrow and thy conception; in sorrow thou shalt bring forth children; and thy desire shall be to thy husband, and he shall rule over thee" (Genesis 3:16). This affects all women today.

Then God punished Adam and his posterity. "Cursed is the land for thy sake, in sorrow shalt thou eat it all the days of thy life" (Genesis 3:17).

God then sent Adam and Eve out of the garden to live for the rest of their lives (Genesis 3:23–24).

Now there is an evolutionary shock wave! The change was sudden due to Adam and Eve's choices or, if you will, the choices our ancestors made.

The choices we make affects our posterity, and without our Heavenly Father's direct guidance, we tend to make a lot of bad decisions in our own individual lives.

Adam and Eve began to follow God's commandments to multiply and replenish the earth. Their children made bad and good choices that affected their posterity, all the way down to us.

Spiritual Evolution Throughout the Ages

The next few pages will look at examples of spiritual evolution with Adam and Eve's children. Pay attention and note how their bad and good choices affected the lives of them and the rest of us all.

Cain and Abel

Adam and Eve's early offspring, Abel, pleased God by making a sacrifice to Him. Cain also made a sacrifice, but God wasn't happy with it. Cain became jealous and killed Abel.

God learns about Cain killing his brother Abel, and as a consequence of his actions, God punished Cain and cursed him "from the earth" (Genesis 4:11). The earth would no longer yield to Cain her strength, and he would be a "fugitive and a vagabond" (Genesis 4:12) on the earth. "And the Lord set a mark upon Cain" (Genesis 15).

Noah

When most of the men and women on the earth had evolved to a wicked state of pleasure and deceit, the Lord decided to destroy all but a few good people (Genesis 6:5–7).

Noah made good choices and was a just man and found grace in the sight of God. As a result, God had Noah and his family build an ark to save them from the flood. The flood was God's way to destroy all the wickedness of man from the earth (Genesis 6:13–22; 7:23, 24).

Noah had evolved to be a good man and all his family were rewarded for his obedience and walked with God (Genesis 6:9; 9:1, 11–13).

Abraham, Isaac, and Jacob

Abraham chose to obey the Lord and was blessed, and God talked with him, saying he would be a father of many nations. God made a covenant with Abraham, and he kept the convent and was blessed along with his posterity (Genesis 17:1–8).

With Isaac, Abraham's son, God would establish an everlasting covenant, and also "with his seed after him" (Genesis 17:19).

Jacob, Isaac's son, is blessed and is called Israel and bears twelve sons that become the twelve tribes of Israel. The Lord indeed blessed Abraham's posterity. However, the children of Israel did come into bondage by the Egyptians, and the children of Israel cried to the Lord and

God remembered his covenant (Exodus 2:23–25).

Moses

Moses was chosen to free the children of Israel from Egypt (Exodus 3:10; 14:21–31).

While Moses was on the mount, the people quickly forgot what the Lord had done and made idols and false gods (Exodus 32:1).

After Moses returned from the mount, he became angry because of the wickedness of the people. Moses had them make a choice, asking, "Who is on the Lord's side?" About three thousand men died when they made their choice to not be on the Lord's side (Exodus 32:19, 26–28).

God destroys the wicked when they're ripe in iniquity and blesses the righteous for his sake while on the earth. After this life, they also receive a just reward for all they do. Good for good and evil for evil.

Sodom and Gomorrah

One example of the wrath of God when people chose wickedness over godliness is the story of the city of Sodom and Gomorrah. The Lord destroys the wicked and saves the righteous (Genesis 18: 20–33).

Abraham knew the city was going to be destroyed and pleaded with the Lord to save the righteous people, knowing his brother–in–law, Lot, was there. Abraham pleaded five times to the Lord. "Peradventure ten shall be found there" to be righteous (Genesis 18:32). The Lord agreed. Lot and his family were led away and saved as the city was being destroyed.

The Tower of Babel and the Jaredite Nation

God also makes changes in our lives when he feels it's for our own good.

An example of this is the Tower of Babel, where God confounded the language of the people (Genesis 11: 1–7).

The Lord not only confounded the language but scattered the people upon the face of all the earth (Genesis 11:8, 9).

In Ether, a record found in the book of Mormon, we read of a group of people, the Jaredites, who were at the Tower of Babel when the languages were changed and the people were scattered over all the earth. The record of Ether states that the brother of Jared was favored of the Lord and cried unto the Lord that he would not confound their language, along with their friends' language. The Lord had compassion upon them (Ether 1: 33–37).

Then the brother of Jared cried unto the Lord about whether they should go, and the Lord had compassion on them, and led them to a choice land, and they raised up a great nation (Ether 1: 39–43).

The people of Jared went northward into the valley of Nimrod and then traveled into the wilderness and built barges and crossed many waters until they reached the seashore and stayed there for the space of four years (Ether 2: 1–14).

Then they built eight barges and set sail on the sea and were blown upon the waters three hundred and forty-four days toward a promised land. They landed upon the shore and grew into a great nation (Ether 6: 1–13).

Many years later, Jaredites became wicked and blood thirsty. Prophets were sent to call them to repentance, and unless they repented, God would destroy them and lead another group over the sea to possess the land of promise (Ether 11: 20–22).

The people did not repent and a great war consumed the land.

The prophet Ether prophesied to Coriantumr, a leader of a great army, telling him to repent. He refused, and Ether said that all would die except Coriantumr, who would live to receive a burial from the new inhabitants of the land (Ether 13: 20–22).

Coriantumr lived while every single one of his people died in battle.

The Nephites and the Lamanites

Many years later, God led a new group of people across the sea. From the book of Mormon, we read of a prophet named Lehi who took his family and departed into the wilderness after he prophesied of the destruction of Jerusalem if the people didn't repent. They did not repent and wanted to take Lehi's life (1 Nephi 1:18–20).

About 600 B.C., the prophet Lehi and his family were led by the hand of the Lord out of the great city Jerusalem. They traveled nearly eastward for the space of eight years until they reached the seashore (1 Nephi 17: 1–6). Then Lehi and his family built a ship and traveled to the promised land, the America continent (1 Nephi 18: 1–25).

This group spread throughout the land. Nephi, one of Lehi's sons, being favored of the Lord, was told to separate from his brethren because they sought to take away his life (2 Nephi 5:2). They became the people of Nephi, or Nephites, a more righteous people, and were blessed for their obedience (2 Nephi 5: 1–11).

The Lord cursed Nephi's brethren for their wickedness, for wanting to take his life. They become known as Laminates, a wicked people. They became "an idle people, full of mischief, subtlety, and did seek in the wilderness for beasts of prey" (2 Nephi 5:24). "They shall be a scourge unto thy seed, to stir them up in remembrance of me; and inasmuch as they will not remember me, and hearken unto my words, they shall scourge them even unto destruction" (verse 25).

Hundreds of years later, history repeats itself because of man's wickedness. Except this time, all the people were not destroyed, only the Nephites.

Mormon, one of the last prophets in the Book of Mormon, wrote to his son, Moroni, during the last great battles of the Nephites and Lamanites (Mormon 6), and testified of their wickedness. "Thou knowest that they are without principle, and past feeling; and their wickedness doth exceed that of the Laminates" (Moroni 9:20). A few verses later, Mormon said, "And if they perish it will be like unto the Jaredites, because of the willfulness of their hearts, seeking for blood and revenge" (verse 23).

We see through these and many more examples that because of our disobedience to God's commandments, we become lost and evolve into natural man in a fallen carnal state, subject to God's punishments.

> For the natural man is an enemy to God, and has been from the fall of Adam, and will be, forever and ever, unless he yields to the enticings of the Holy Spirit, and putteth off the natural man and becometh a saint through the atonement of Christ the Lord, and becometh as a child, submissive, meek, humble, patient, full of love, willing to submit to all things which the Lord seeth fit to inflict upon him, even as a child doth submit to his father (Mosiah 3: 19).

> But the natural man receiveth not the things of the Spirit of God: for they are foolishness unto him: neither can he know them, because they are spiritually discerned (1 Corinthians 2: 14).

The idea of a God in heaven requires faith in something unseen yet felt spirit to spirit. A great example is electricity. Let's say we have a large unlimited source of power, and until we plug something into it and complete the circuit, nothing happens. That power or kinetic energy just sits there, looking for a place to go.

Similarly, our Heavenly Father's spiritual influence from the Holy Ghost is waiting for us to complete the circuit so He can enhance and illuminate our lives with knowledge and truth to help guide us back to God's presence.

Remember, we need to chase the Holy Ghost to learn truth. We do this through our faithful actions, charity toward all mankind, prayer, fasting, and scripture study.

For how knoweth a man the master whom he has not served, and who is a stranger unto him, and is far from the thoughts and intents of his heart? (Mosiah 5:13)

To Love

Learning how to love can be hard for some. To love is to give of oneself to another, which is learned through trial and error, and is a hard thing to do because it hurts so much—so much so that many would rather just love themselves so they can't get hurt. But what they don't see is how much going without love really affects their lives and the lives around them.

Life without love is meaningless, being void of emotions that emulate the true meaning and purpose of Christ's birth, death, and resurrection.

To love is to obey all things.

Richard L. Bigford

To love is to forgive all.

To love is to be gentle to all.

To love is to be kind to all.

To love is to be patient with all.

To love is to take advice from all.

To love is to listen to all.

To love is to give all of oneself—body, mind, and spirit—as our Savior, our older brother did for us, that we might live again with our Father in Heaven.

True love is unselfish and gives to all these things and more.

True love goes the extra mile and suffers to an extent even as Christ has suffered for us.

True love is the guide to obedience, understanding, knowledge, and freedom.

True love overcomes all these things and more.

An Evolution of Faith

It all starts with a prayer to open the doors to true life and love.

Richard L. Bigford

What Has Sin Got To Do With It?

Well, to start with, whether we believe it or not, we all sin. It's hard to admit that we sin, because when we do, we ultimately admit that we've made a mistake, and we don't like admitting that we're not perfect. Admitting this makes us seem inferior to others by showing our weaknesses and making us vulnerable to criticism.

No one likes to be criticized. It makes us feel as if we are being picked on. True criticism should build us up and help us become a better person to prepare us for more of life's challenges.

So one way or another, we have broken one of the ten basic commandments God has given us through a prophet of God, yea, from Moses! Such things have been given from God. Remember, Moses broke the first tablets of a higher law that we weren't ready for.

So to me, since we all sin, if we repent and do that sin no more, and learn and grow from our mistakes, it can be a stepping stone to perfection—through much effort and prayer, on your knees, if you dare.

The Borrower

Thou shalt not steal or commit anything like unto it. If one borrows something, one should try to return it in a timely manner. Sure, things happen, and sometimes we forget, but think of how you feel when you loan something out and it never comes back.

If something never gets returned, then it is considered stolen or lost, depending on the lender's disposition on how he or she views the situation. The loner has all rights to what is his or her property whether or not you are done with it. Borrowing and not returning has created so much mistrust and dishonesty. It's not worth it. Just return it in a timely manner so you don't forget whose property it really is.

Just think of all the things we take or borrow from our Heavenly father and never return or even give thanks to Him for letting us borrow it. For all things are His to give with love untamed.

We are all borrowers in life. So let us be thankful for what we have been given, through almighty prayer and supplication to our God above, with sincere truth and love. Amen.

Thou Shalt Remember and Honor Him

It's important to remember God in all things. In order to remember God in all things, one must revere him through mighty supplication by studying, searching, and pondering all God's words that are given through his prophets of old and his prophet in these latter days. And praying and studying more than just once a week, or whenever a whim appears.

Remember, dedication shows commitment, and commitment leads to obedience, and obedience shows love to one's desires.

Richard L. Bigford

I don't know about you, but I desire to return to heaven and live with my Holiest of Gods, yea, even my Heavenly Father of whom I adore. Amen!

My Lost Soul

My lost soul is mine to tame and unite with my body, in perfect harmony with God's laws, to rescue and pull up from the lake of the sands of time that surrounds the holy mansion high on the hill. That is a journey so hard to climb and find the way that one needs a helping hand from the Good Shepherd to teach us how to avoid being pulled by the temptation to swim in the oasis amidst the heat of the day, to give the illusion you're okay, and only you know the way.

Once you become seduced by temptation's power, your soul becomes hidden in the sands of time. To truly find your soul again, one must ever so quietly listen to the voice of the Good

Shepherd as the sand gently tumbles as souls are being sifted, dug, and measured and twisted, and even more.

So many people are looking for their souls and much more. It's important to help other people as you look for your soul as they find their souls. It's one less soul you have to sift through to find your own.

When all souls are found and in their right place, the sands of time will become transparent from the heat of busy feet, which is turned into a beautiful lake of glass that will forever last, capturing the events of the past.

Final Thoughts

One last encouragement from the book of Mormon.

> Therefore, cheer up your hearts, and remember that ye are free to act for yourselves—to choose the way of everlasting death or the way of eternal life (2 Nephi 10:23).

In the book of Mormon, we read of the wellbeing of thousands of souls who died and returned home to our Heavenly Father after a great battle.

> And in one year were thousands and tens of thousands of souls sent to the eternal

world, that they might reap their rewards according to their works, whether they were good or whether they were bad, to reap eternal happiness or eternal misery, according to the spirit which they listed to obey, whether it be a good spirit or a bad one (Alma 3:26).

Wherefore, my beloved brethren, reconcile yourselves to the will of God, and not to the will of the devil and the flesh; and remember, after ye are reconciled unto God, that it is only in and through the grace of God that ye are saved.

Wherefore, may God raise you from death by the power of the resurrection, and also from everlasting death by the power of the atonement, that ye may be received into the eternal kingdom of God, that ye may praise him through grace divine. Amen. (2 Nephi 10:23–25).

I give my testimony that we all will evolve to a state of everlasting happiness with God, or to a state of endless misery and torment with Satan, depending on our choices in this life. So evolve well, my beloved brothers and sisters. Your happiness or misery depends on you. It's my prayer that you make a choice of everlasting happiness and reconcile your life with God through repentance, and pray always for forgiveness and mercy! May God's grace be upon us all, in and through His Beloved Son Jesus Christ. Amen.

Richard L. Bigford

66

A Collection of Poems

by Richard L. Bigford

Richard L. Bigford

To Live in a Barn

To tell a tall tale, to spin a small yarn,
Believe it or not, I lived in a barn!

Outside a small town, in a place not far
from where I now stay,
My mother owned a house where I
used to play back in the day.

One day while we were all away from
our home,
While we did roam,
Something went down
That was the talk of the town.

With a spark here and a spark there.
Soon there was fire everywhere.
It was all gone in one day.
What more is there to say?

With no house, oh, what to do?
We surely couldn't live in a shoe.
My mother did think, then she did do,

She must have been inspired by a moo.

To the barn, we did go.
There was no other place to really go.
We shoveled all that day.
I do believe we forgot to pray.

About six months did go by,
Before a new trailer Mom did buy.
Time went by, and life was now good.

But soon it became another matter.
The trailer was small and couldn't get
any fatter.

More room we did need,
More moved in that we had to feed.
With not much room on the floor,
Someone had to move out once more.

So I somehow knew what to do.
I must have been inspired by the moo,
too.
Off to the barn I did move in to stay.

An Evolution of Faith

It's something I will remember even yet
today.

I took a corner of the barn and made it
my home.
This is where I did roam.

With one wall of solid cement,
And the floor, too,
And three walls of wood.
It was all good.

I laid it with carpet all over to insulate.
To turn back, it was too late.
I pimped it out with a water bed.
It was the best time I ever had.

Though the winters were sometimes
cold,
And perhaps even a little mold,
It's a story that deserves to be told,
Precious to me even more than gold.

Richard L. Bigford

My Wife, Part of My Life

I once knew my love, and she knew me.
Together, we signed up for eternity.
Tick tick, time went so quick and did so
softly slip away,
We didn't know what to do or say.

With one, two, three, yet four.
They were delivered at our door.
Then my wife said no more.
Oh, how I wish I had some more.

Shortly thereafter the deed was done.
Something did happen that I told no
one.
That I held in my heart for such a long
time,
That I let you know at this moment in
time.

One night, I wake up from my sleep,
From the sound of a lost sheep.

Little and brave did she seem to be
As she spoke to me.

With a vision in my head,
This little girl was by my bed.
The sounds of what she had said
Will always be in my head.

Daddy, Daddy, she had said,
As she stood by my bed.
Where is the little girl who makes me
cry?
Will I see her before I die?

During our time together,
There was some very stormy weather.
Yet the question of what held us
together
For such a long, long time.

Twenty-seven years, we softly went
through.
Oh Lord, I just don't know what to do.
She's the one who kept me true.

An Evolution of Faith

Life started us together,
With all sorts of silly weather.

Amidst the trials, old and new,
We just didn't know really what to do.
So separate we did do.

There was no more I love you,
Just a passing wave or two.
This is what we chose to do.
Good luck to both me and you.

Richard L. Bigford

Once More, To Love and Adore

Now I look yet once more
For the one I wish to adore.
I tried to date,
With the idea it's never too late.
I just couldn't wait for fate.

But with not knowing what to do,
I was a kid not knowing how to tie his
shoe.

So I hoped online.

I set the bait.
That is where I did wait.

My eyes did see many across the open
sea.
But which one is meant for me?

Even though I couldn't wait,
I still had to rely on the hand of fate.

Richard L. Bigford

But yet wait!
Perhaps I didn't have the right bait.

Then all of a sudden, out of the blue,
A twitch, a twiggle,
My bait did wiggle.

I took my stance so proud and true.
I was ready to say I love you.

Oh, so pretty, could this be she,
The one meant to be for me?

I did try so hard to impress.
I did all but wear a very funny dress.
It turned out to be just a mess.

Without trying longer to get to know,
It sure was the wrong way to go.

I made myself look like a fool.
I sure did lose my hope, my cool.
Just like when I was in high school.

An Evolution of Faith

I did take a short break.
This job is not a piece of cake.
Perhaps I should try a different lake,
A smaller size with no wake.

In time, after a short boo-hoo,
I realized what now to do.

Don't make such a clatter.
Just be you! It doesn't matter.

Fate will come in its own time,
With no reason or no rhyme.
But always comes at the right time.

Richard L. Bigford

An Evolution of Faith

To Kill? Or Not To Kill? Is The Question at Hand.

In life, all things die.
Quite often we wonder why.
Yes, the good and the bad.
It quite often is so sad.

But life goes on, the tempest twirls,
With ever more fervent swirls.
So grab what you can, grab what you
may,
Live to fight another day.

If we should land on a bended knee,
Oh please, let God guide you and me.

To kill a tree, is this meant to be?
To kill a bug and sweep it under a rug.
To kill to eat such sweet, raw meat.
To kill a fruit for loving a flavor.
Surely, all things we must savor.

Richard L. Bigford

Isn't it all laid before our feet?
Yes, all things are sent to me and you.
To hear, to smell, to taste
Please don't waste!

To touch, to feel,
Is this life really real?
According to what we want to see,
This world is meant for you and me.

All things seem to feed one another.
 Just don't kill thine sister, brother,
father, or mother.
We just need to learn how to live with
one another.

So use your discretion when life is
yours to take.For heaven's sake!

Life revolves around all things big or
small.
Please try to remember them all.
Let us get along with what we just need.

An Evolution of Faith

Try not to develop that nasty habit of greed.

Richard L. Bigford

Acknowledgments

Lisa Rector, I could never thank you enough for your editing skills. You did an amazing job at organizing my thoughts, and correcting my grammar.

Thanks, Julie Spencer for your kind words of advice to help me get this far in writing a book, and your outstanding skills as an editor. I'm grateful to have you as a friend.

Thank you Amanda—the lady who is the new chapter in my life. I know you will help me grow in so many ways.

Most especially, thank you to God and to my children, and family. You are my inspiration.

-Richard L. Bigford

Richard L. Bigford

About the Author

Richard L. Bigford began his journey of faith when he was young. He was molded by God's gentle hands through life experiences despite being raised in a divorced family. He saw his father on weekends but spent most of his time on a small farm. At age eleven, Richard developed cancer, fought it, and survived. He was baptized a member of The Church of Jesus Christ of Latter-day Saints at fifteen, and later served a mission for the Church in the Florida Jacksonville Mission. His marriage brought four kids, though he divorced after twenty-seven years. One of the most memorable experiences Richard had was to baptize his grandfather in his older years.

Richard is devoted to this life, the Church, and those around him through service. His only desire is to follow in the Savior's footsteps. He is constantly learning about God's creations on earth and the beauty of them all. Richard hopes his writings will strengthen, comfort, and guide others on their journey through this mortal life as they strive to live with their Eternal Father in Heaven